GOOD DOG POEMS

GOOD DOG
POEMS

Compiled by
William Cole

Illustrated by Ruth Sanderson

CHARLES SCRIBNER'S SONS | NEW YORK

Copyright © 1981 William Cole

Library of Congress Cataloging in Publication Data
Cole, William, date   Good dog poems.
Includes index.
1. Dogs—Poetry.   2. English, poetry.
3. American poetry.   I. Sanderson, Ruth.
II. Title.
PR1195.D65C6   1980   821'.008'036   80-21547
ISBN 0-684-16709-3

1 3 5 7 9 11 13 15 17 19 QD/C 20 18 16 14 12 10 8 6 4 2

Printed in the United States of America

ACKNOWLEDGMENTS

The Editor and Publishers gratefully acknowledge the following poets, agents, and publishers for permission to reprint poems in this anthology. Every effort has been made to locate all persons having any rights or interests in the material published here. If some acknowledgments have not been made, their omission is unintentional and is regretted.

"Whippet" by Prudence Andrew. Reprinted by permission of the author and Macmillan London Ltd.

"The Bloodhound," "The Collies," and "The Dachshund" by Edward Anthony from *Every Dog Has His Say*. Copyright © 1947, 1975, by Watson-Guptill Publications, Inc., New York, NY. Reprinted by permission of Watson-Guptill Publications.

"Hector the Dog" by Kate Barnes. Reprinted by permission; © 1961 The New Yorker Magazine, Inc.

"Brave Rover" by Max Beerbohm reprinted by permission of The Stephen Greene Press from *Max in Verse: Rhymes and Parodies by Max Beerbohm*,

Contents

Forepause

People can get pretty silly about dogs and write awful poems about them. None here, I hasten to add! But they get very sentimental and cute. I have two old books devoted to poems about dogs. And devoted is the right word—the dogs seem to own the people instead of the people owning the dogs. I've got one of these books before me. I open it at random, and here's the first line of the poem that faces me: "O small black puppy with angel eyes . . . ." Angel eyes? What in the world are angel eyes? And on a dog! It's OK to love a dog, but don't get dopey about it.

One of the great things about dogs is how different they are from one another. There are mean dogs, and half-mean dogs, and friendly ones, and want-to-be-friendly ones, brave ones, stupid ones—just like people. Traditionally, different breeds have different personality traits: poodles and German shepherds are intelligent, chows are snappish, Irish setters are flighty, dobermans are dangerous—but of course there are exceptions in each case.

I have a dog, Jimmy. A mutt—but beautiful. In a funny way he shares the characteristics of every breed that's in him. In some ways he's brave—especially if a strange male dog invades his territory. Sometimes he's cowardly—if he challenges a strange large dog and gets beaten. In some ways he's an awful faker. If he's in the car with me and sees another dog outside the car—my, but he's fierce! Barking, snarling, using terrible language, raising a hullabaloo, and fogging up the windows. It's all show, protecting me and the car—from a safe position. He's also quite gentlemanly; when we let him out and he wants to come in again, he sits outside the front door and gives a discreet bark. A very special bark that he doesn't use other times. It means, "Let me in, please." If nobody responds right away, he's patient and lets three or four minutes elapse before he gives another yap. And he's funny—most dogs are. When he's resting, which he does most of the time, you can press his rib cage gently but firmly and he'll go uuuuuuh! A wonderful groan. Everyone in the household presses his rib cage from time to time, and he doesn't seem to mind.

But enough about my dog; I could go on for pages about his peculiarities. I like all dogs and speak to any I meet, especially those tied up outside a store. These are usually quite uneasy and don't take their eyes away from the store entrance. I like to stop and reassure them that they haven't been deserted. "It's OK," I say, "the boss will be out soon." Sometimes they flicker a worried look at me and give a small wag. But their total interest is on that door. No other animal ever concentrates so intently.

It is interesting to see the amount of amused affection that comes through in these poems. Something you don't find in poems about cats or horses. Affection, yes. But not amused affection. Dogs are funny and lovable, and—I hope you agree—wonderful subjects for poetry.

WILLIAM COLE

PUPPIES

The Young Puppy

There was a young puppy called Howard,
Who at fighting was rather a coward;
   He never quite ran
   When the battle began,
But he started at once to bow-wow hard.

A. A. MILNE

Little tiny puppy dog
Sleeping soundly like a log
Better wake him for his dinner
Or else he'll start to sleep much thinner.

SPIKE MILLIGAN

Poetic Tale

Oh give me a pup
Whose long tail turns up
In an arc like a banner unfurled,
And wags willy-nilly,
Ecstatic and silly,
En rapport with an elegant world!

Whose caudal appendage
(That eloquent endage!)
Builds personality plus,
As in ardent rendition,
And sans inhibition
It waggles its far terminus.

Give me no squabtail,
No abbreviate bobtail,
No half-expressed tail of devotion!
I want my dog finished,
Complete, undiminished,
Unabridged in both inches and motion.

With a tail made for flailing!
Away with cur-tailing!
Give me passionate, frenzied zigzagging,
Of tails that are built for,
Tails set atilt for
Wagging!

GRACE MADDOCK MILLER

Remarks from the Pup

She's taught me that I mustn't bark
   At little noises after dark,
But just refrain from any fuss
   Until I'm sure they're dangerous.
This would be easier, I've felt,
   If noises could be seen or smelt.

She's very wise, I have no doubt,
   And plans ahead what she's about;
Yet after eating, every day,
   She throws her nicest bones away.
If she were really less obtuse
   She'd bury them for future use.

But that which makes me doubt the most
   Those higher powers that humans boast
Is not so much a fault like that,
   Nor yet her fondness for the cat,
But on our pleasant country strolls
   Her dull indifference to holes!

Ah me! what treasures might be found
   In holes that lead to underground!
However vague or small one is,
   It sends me into ecstasies;
While she, alas! stands by to scoff,
   Or meanly comes to call me off.

Oh, if I once had time to spend
   To reach a hole's extremest end,
I'd grab it fast, without a doubt,
   And promptly pull it inside out;
Then drag it home with all my power
   To chew on in a leisure hour.

Of all the mistresses there are,
   Mine is the loveliest by far!
For would I wag myself apart
   If I could thus reveal my heart.
But on some things, I must conclude
   Mine is the saner attitude.

BURGES JOHNSON

Wonder

Collie puppies in a dooryard,
Wheeling along lopsided,
So hard to manage those hind legs,
Standing, blue eyes on nothing,
Noses twitching,
Stubby tails in the air,
Trying to remember what they are thinking about:

Fat puppies that forget everything,
Even the terrible
White teeth their mother yops at them
When she eats her supper:

Fat puppies full of wonder
At round holes where spiders live,
At the wide wings of a yellow butterfly,
And lifting shrill voices of wonder
At the stranger who leans over their gate
Making uncouth noises.

BERNARD RAYMUND

Puppy

Puppy is one I've failed with; he came too close
to a predecessor who left a void of affection
Puppy could never fill.

His mother was collie,
his father nondescript, and Puppy is some of both.
His fur is yellow-red with a fine white collar,
but his head's too small for his body
and his brain power's lacking. He's sly enough
to slip away unobserved to the next farm
where the dogs are, but not much more.

All of him went to affection; it oozes from him
like cider from crushed apples; all he wants
is to put his head on your knee and rest.

And little enough he gets from life:
a chance sometimes to chase the fence-jumper Lena
back in the pasture or out of the haystack,
or a stray cat out of the yard. He's no good
with sheep; he chases them any direction
they happen to run, out of the barn
as well as in, being content to chase
whatever runs, or even content to chase nothing
around the barn as fast as his legs will go.
He was born useless and somehow seems to know it.
His life is a long round of unsatisfied desire.
His heaven would be a place where all day long
he'd lay his head upon somebody's knees.

FRED LAPE

DOGGONE
FUNNY DOGS

The Dog

The truth I do not stretch or shove
When I state the dog is full of love.
I've also proved, by actual test,
A wet dog is the lovingest.

OGDEN NASH

Dog Wanted

I don't want a dog that is wee and effeminate,
Fluffy and peevish and coyly discriminate;
Yapping his wants in querulous tone,
Preferring a cake to a good honest bone.

I don't want a beast that is simply enormous,
Making me feel as obscure as a dormouse
Whenever he hurtles with jubilant paws
On my shoulders, and rips with his powerful
    claws
My sturdiest frocks; the kind of a mammal
That fits in a parlor as well as a camel,

That makes the floor shake under foot when he
    treads,
And bumps into tables and bounds over beds.

The sort of a pet that I have in my mind
Is a dog of the portable, washable kind;
Not huge and unwieldy, not frilly and silly,
Not sleek and not fuzzy, not fawning, not chilly—
A merry, straightforward, affectionate creature
Who likes me as playmate, respects me as teacher,
And thumps with his tail when he sees me come
    near
As gladly as if I'd been gone for a year;
Whose eyes, when I praise him, grow warm with
    elation;
Whose tail droops in shame at my disapprobation;
No pedigreed plaything to win me a cup—
Just a portable, washable, lovable pup!

MARGARET MACKPRANG MACKAY

On Buying a Dog

"I wish to buy a dog," she said,
"A dog you're sure is quite well bred,
In fact, I'd like some guarantee
He's favored with a pedigree."

"My charming friend," the pet man said,
"I have a dog that's so well bred,
If he could talk, I'll guarantee
He'd never speak to you or me."

EDGAR KLAUBER

Montgomery *(With acknowledgments to T. S. Eliot's Macavity)*

There's lots of funny goings-on the public don't
     suspect,
A deal of dark and dirty deeds detectives don't de-
     tect;
There's many a pampered pussy gets garrotted
     when it's smoggy,
Or frightened into kittens by some prowling dirty
     doggy.
And all these crimes, committed in the daytime or
     at night
Are sweet as marrow bones to *him* and fill him
     with delight.

But what is he? And who is he? The moniker's
     Montgomery.
He thinks pet poodles, lapdogs, pugs, just flum-
     mery and mummery;

He's Montgomery the Monstrous, slimmest dog be-
   neath the sky;
The cur behind cur-riminals, the jinx on F.B.I.

When juicy steaks are pinched or pussies hounded
   to despair
And cops arrive to find the crook, Montgomery's
   not there.
All this is most mysterious and I'm sure you're
   wondering how
He never gives himself away by paw-print or bow-
   wow.
But we can tell the secret that so baffles the police,
How Montgomery indulges his cur-riminal caprice.

For have you noticed all the doggies, everywhere
   you turn,
So blandly trotting past you with an air of uncon-
   cern?
Be they pedigree or mongrel, vicious vagabonds or
   fops,
They are all on secret missions for Montgomery the
   Tops.

H. A. C. EVANS

Motto for a Dog House

I love this little house because
  It offers, after dark,
A pause for rest, a rest for paws,
  A place to moor my bark.

ARTHUR GUITERMAN

Daley's Dorg Wattle

"You can talk about yer sheep dorgs," said the
    man from Allan's Creek,
"But I know a dorg that simply knocked 'em
    bandy!—
Do whatever you would show him, and you'd
    hardly need to speak;
Owned by Daley, drover cove in Jackandandy.

"We was talkin' in the parlour, me and Daley,
    quiet like,
When a blow-fly starts a-buzzin' round the ceilin',
Up gets Daley, and he says to me, 'You wait a
    minute, Mike,
And I'll show you what a dorg he is at heelin'.'

15

"And an empty pickle-bottle was a-standin' on the
  shelf,
Daley takes it down and puts it on the table,
And he bets me drinks that blinded dorg would do
  it by himself—
And I didn't think as how as he was able!

"Well, he shows the dorg the bottle, and he points
  up to the fly,
And he shuts the door, and says to him—'Now
  Wattle!'
And in less than fifteen seconds, spare me days, it
  ain't a lie,
That there dorg has got that inseck in the bottle."

W. T. GOODGE

Suzie's New Dog

Your dog? What dog? You mean it?—that!
  I was about to leave a note
Pinned to a fish to warn my cat
  To watch for a mouse in an overcoat!

So that's a dog! Is it any breed
  That anyone ever knew—or guessed?
Oh, a Flea Terrier! Yes indeed.
  Well now, I *am* impressed!

16

I guess no robber will try your house
   Or even cut through your yard.
Not when he knows you have a mouse
   —I mean a dog—like that on guard!

You have to go? I'm glad you came!
   I don't see a thing like that
Just every day. Does it have a name?
   Fang, eh? Well, I must warn my cat.

JOHN CIARDI

Pourquoi

O Jean Baptiste, pourquoi,
O Jean Baptiste, pourquoi,
O Jean Baptiste,
Pourquoi you greased
My little dog's nose with tar?

Your little dog had catarrh,
Your little dog had catarrh,
And that was the reason
Why I have greasen
Your little dog's nose with tar.

O Jean Baptiste, I'm glad,
O Jean Baptiste, I'm glad,
O Jean Baptiste,
I'm glad you greased
My little dog's nose with tar.

ANONYMOUS

Canine Amenities

Said the fur-coated dame to the hairless pup,
"You cute little thing, let me cover you up!"
Said the pup, "Were *you* dressed in your birthday
    suit
You'd be colder than I and not half as cute!"

ANONYMOUS

Brave Rover

Rover killed the goat,
He bit him through the throat,
And when it all was over
The goat's ghost haunted Rover.

And yet (the plot here thickens)
Rover killed the chickens.
They thought he was a fox—
And then he killed the cocks.

And now events moved faster:
Rover killed his master,
And then he took the life
Of his late master's wife.

And we must not forget he
Killed Rachel and killed Bettie,
Then Billie and then John.
How dogs do carry on!

To Bradford he repaired.
His great white teeth he bared
And then, with awful snarls,
Polished off Uncle Charles.

Albert in London trembled—
An aspen he resembled—
His life he held not cheap
And wept. (I heard him weep.)

Brave Rover heard him too.
He knew full well who's who,
And entered with a grin
The Fields of Lincoln's Inn.

The Elysian Fields begin
Near those of Lincoln's Inn.
'Tis there that Albert's gone.
How dogs do carry on!

MAX BEERBOHM

Lincoln's Inn: Courts of law in London
Elysian Fields: Heaven

The Ambiguous Dog

The dog beneath the cherry-tree
Has ways that sorely puzzle me:

Behind, he wags a friendly tail;
Before, his growl would turn you pale!

His meaning isn't plain and clear;
Oh, is the wag or growl sincere?

I think I'd better not descend;
His bite is at the growly end.

ARTHUR GUITERMAN

Confession of a Glutton

after i ate my dinner then i ate
part of a shoe
i found some archies by a bathroom pipe
and ate them too
i ate some glue
i ate a bone that had got nice and ripe
six weeks buried in the ground
i ate a little mousie that i found
i ate some sawdust from the cellar floor
it tasted sweet
i ate some outcast meat
and some roach paste by the pantry door
and then the missis had some folks to tea
nice folks who petted me
and so i ate
cakes from a plate
i ate some polish that they use
for boots and shoes
and then i went back to the missis swell tea party
i guess i must have eat too hearty
of something maybe cake
for then came the earthquake
you should have seen the missis face
and when the boss came in she said
no wonder that dog hangs his head
he knows hes in disgrace

i am a well intentioned little pup
but sometimes things come up
to get a little dog in bad
and now i feel so very very sad
but the boss said never mind old scout
time wears disgraces out

DON MARQUIS

archies: cockroaches

Verse for a Certain Dog

Such glorious faith as fills your limpid eyes,
   Dear little friend of mine, I never knew.
All-innocent are you, and yet all-wise.
   (For Heaven's sake, stop worrying that shoe!)
You look about, and all you see is fair;
   This mighty globe was made for you alone.
Of all the thunderous ages, you're the heir.
   (Get off the pillow with that dirty bone!)

A skeptic world you face with steady gaze;
   High in young pride you hold your noble head;
Gayly you meet the rush of roaring days.

(*Must* you eat puppy biscuit on the bed?)
Lancelike your courage, gleaming swift and strong,
   Yours the white rapture of a wingéd soul,
Yours is a spirit like a May-day song.
   (God help you, if you break the goldfish bowl!)

"Whatever is, is good"—your gracious creed.
   You wear your joy of living like a crown.
Love lights your simplest act, your every deed.
   (Drop it, I tell you—put that kitten down!)
You are God's kindliest gift of all—a friend.
   Your shining loyalty unflecked by doubt,
You ask but leave to follow to the end.
   (Couldn't you wait until I took you out?)

DOROTHY PARKER

I've got a dog as thin as a rail,
He's got fleas all over his tail;
Every time his tail goes flop,
The fleas on the bottom all hop to the top.

ANONYMOUS

23

ROUGH DOGS,
TOUGH DOGS

Big Dog

Big Dog,
my God what I cannot know,
and you by God will never learn:
Eighteen feet straight down out the barn;
not a fall, a leap! And the aching wait
while you pawed the empty air for ground
that wasn't there, and hit . . .

(Big Dog, your jaw a bloody plow)

And I stumbled below to find you swaying
on those great paws, to praise your head
in my cradled knees, and to steady, steady,
that strange dog mind.

(Big Dog, whose size and run are wolf)

It would have broken ten men in two, but you
—whose wet tongue would, had I fallen,
have done what I could not do—you lie whole,
asleep in quivering dream of the slow sheep
you herd to barn.

Big Dog
in off the street, at the marrow
may all your stolen bones be sweet.

PHILIP BOOTH

The Train Dogs

Out of the night and the north;
    Savage of breed and of bone,
Shaggy and swift comes the yelping band,
Freighters of fur from the voiceless land
    That sleeps in the Arctic zone.

Laden with skins from the north,
    Beaver and bear and raccoon,
Marten and mink from the polar belts,
Otter and ermine and sable pelts—
    The spoils of the hunter's moon.

Out of the night and the north,
    Sinewy, fearless and fleet,
Urging the pack through the pathless snow,
The Indian driver, calling low,
    Follows with moccasined feet.

Ships of the night and the north,
    Freighters on prairies and plains,
Carrying cargoes from field and flood
They scent the trail through their wild red blood,
    The wolfish blood in their veins.

PAULINE JOHNSON

Tim, an Irish Terrier

It's wonderful dogs they're breeding now:
Small as a flea or large as a cow
But my old lad Tim he'll never be bet
By any dog that ever he met.
"Come on," says he, "for I'm not kilt yet."

No matter the size of the dog he'll meet,
Tim trails his coat the length o' the street.
D'ye mind his scars an' his ragged ear,
The like of a Dublin Fusilier?
He's a massacree dog that knows no fear.

But he'd stick to me till his latest breath;
An' he'd go with me to the gates of death.

29

He'd wait for a thousand years, maybe,
Scratching the door an' whining for me
If myself were inside in Purgatory.

So I laugh when I hear thim make it plain
That dogs and men never meet again.
For all their talk who'd listen to thim,
With the soul in the shining eyes of him?
Would God be wasting a dog like Tim?

W. M. LETTS

Lone Dog

I'm a lean dog, a keen dog, a wild dog, and lone;
I'm a rough dog, a tough dog, hunting on
    my own;
I'm a bad dog, a mad dog, teasing silly sheep;
I love to sit and bay the moon, to keep fat souls
    from sleep.

I'll never be a lap dog, licking dirty feet,
A sleek dog, a meek dog, cringing for my meat,
Not for me the fireside, the well-filled plate,
But shut door, and sharp stone, and cuff and kick
    and hate.

Not for me the other dogs, running by my side,
Some have run a short while, but none of them
    would bide.
O mine is still the lone trail, the hard trail, the
    best,
Wide wind, and wild stars, and hunger of the
    quest!

IRENE RUTHERFORD MCLEOD

Scroppo's Dog

In the early morning, past the shut houses,
past the harbor shut in fog, I walk free and
single. It is summer—that's lucky. The whole
day is mine. At the end of our village I stop
to greet Scroppo's dog, whose chain is wrapped
around a large dusty boulder. His black coat
is gray, from crouching every day in the gravel
of Scroppo's yard—a yard by a scrap-filled pond,
where Scroppo deals in wrecked cars and car
    parts.
I guess he gets them from crashes on the express-
    way,
or from abandoned junks he loots by the roadside.

31

I don't know the name of Scroppo's dog. I remem-
   ber
him, years ago, as a big fierce-looking pup.
It may have been his first day chained there,
or shortly after, that he first greeted me:
his eyes big nuggets shooting orange sparks, his
red tongue rippling out between clean fangs—
fangs as white as lilies of the valley that bloom
in a leafy border by Scroppo's weathered porch.
It was late May, as now, when with sudden joyful
bark, black fur erect and gleaming, the dog
rushed toward me—but was stopped by his chain,
a chain then bright and new. I would have met
and stroked him, but didn't dare get near him,
in his strangled frenzy—in his unbelief—
that something at his throat cut short
his coming, going, leaping, circling, running—
something he couldn't bite through, tripped him:
he could go only so far: to the trash in the weeds
at the end of the driveway, to the edge
of the oily, broken cement in back, where
      Scroppo's
muddy flatbed truck stands at night.

Now, as I walk toward him, the dog growls,
then cowers back. He is old and fat and dirty,
and his eyes spit equal hate and fear.
He knows exactly how far he can strain

from the rock and the wrapped chain. There's
a trench in a circle in the oily dirt his paws
have dug. Days and weeks and months and years
of summer heat and winter cold have been
    survived
within the radius of that chain.
Scroppo's dog knows me, and wants to come and
touch. At the same time, his duty to expel
the intruder makes him bare his teeth and
bristle. He pounds his matted tail, he snarls
while cringing, alternately stretches toward me,
and springs back. His bark, husky and cracked,
follows me for a block, until I turn the corner,
crossing the boundary of the cove.

I've never touched Scroppo's dog, and his
yearning tongue has never licked me. Yet, we
know each other well. Subject to the seasons'
extremes, confined to the limits of our yard,
early fettered by an obscure master in whose
power we bask, bones grow frail while steel
thickens; while rock fattens, passions and
senses pale. Scroppo's dog sniffs dust.
He sleeps a lot. My nose grown blunt, I need
to remember the salty damp of the air's taste
on summer mornings, first snowfall's freshness,
the smoke of burning leaves. Each midday,
when the firehouse whistle blows, a duet

of keen, weird howls is heard, as, at the steep
edge of hopelessness, with muzzle pointed,
ears flat, eyes shut, Scroppo's dog forlornly
yodels in time to the village siren sounding noon.

MAY SWENSON

HOUNDS AND
HUNTERS

from **A Midsummer Night's Dream**

My hounds are bred out of the Spartan kind,
So flewed, so sanded; and their heads are hung
With ears that sweep away the morning dew;
Crook-kneed, and dew-lapped like Thessalian
    bulls,
Slow in pursuit, but matched in mouth like bells,
Each unto each. A cry more tunable
Was never hollaed to, nor cheered with horn,
In Crete, in Sparta, nor in Thessaly:
Judge when you hear.

WILLIAM SHAKESPEARE

Rake

There's no better dog nor Hardcastle's Rake:
Not a hundred guineas would Hardcastle take
For his wall-eyed dog: an' Ben is a man
Who takes good money whenever he can!
But Rake's worth more to him nor brass,
An' Hardcastle luves him more nor his lass

Nor his bairns: at least so our neebors say:
An' his owd lass laughs wi', "Happen, he may;
But our bairns are fed by a sheep-dog's work,
An' Rake is a dog 'at niver 'ull shirk;
On a winter's neet he'll snore on t'hearth,
An' at slightest stir in t'fold or t'garth
He's at our Ben's side; togither they 'ull go
Out on t'moor in hail or snow;
An' some hours later they'll baith coom in
Tired an' famished, an' dirty as sin . . .
When our Ben goes on his last lang trudge,
Doon t'Valley o' Death, thro' rain an' sludge,
An' wins at last to t'Gowden Gate,
Theer'll be trouble in Heaven if Rake, his mate,
Can't pass; our Ben 'ull rampage an' shout
If ony saint shuts his sheep-dog out;
If Peter refuses to have him? By gow!
At yon gate theer'll be a hell of a row!"

DOROTHY UNA RATCLIFFE

The Hound

The hound was cuffed, the hound was kicked,
O' the ears was cropped, o' the tail was nicked,
(All.)   Oo-hoo-o, howled the hound.
The hound into his kennel crept;

He rarely wept, he never slept.
His mouth he always open kept,
    Licking his bitter wound,
      The hound,
(All.)   U-lu-lo, howled the hound.

A star upon his kennel shone
That showed the hound a meat-bare bone.
(All.)   O hungry was the hound!
The hound had but a churlish wit:
He seized the bone, he crunched, he bit.
"An thou wert Master, I had slit
    Thy throat with a huge wound,"
      Quo' hound.
(All.)   O angry was the hound.

The star in castle-windows shone,
The Master lay abed, alone.
(All.)   Oh ho, why not? quo' hound.
He leapt, he seized the throat, he tore
The Master, head from neck, to floor,
And rolled the head i' the kennel door,
    And fled and salved his wound,
      Good hound!
(All.)   U-lu-lo, howled the hound.

SIDNEY LANIER

The Rabbit Hunter

Careless and still
The hunter lurks
With gun depressed,
Facing alone
The alder swamps
Ghastly snow-white.
And his hound works
In the offing there
Like one possessed,
And yelps delight
And sings and romps,
Bringing him on
The shadowy hare
For him to rend
And deal a death
That he nor it
(Nor I) have wit
To comprehend.

ROBERT FROST

Hound on the Church Porch

The farmer knew each time a friend went past
Though he was deep in Sunday and his eyes
Were on the preacher or the azure squares
The high church sashes cut out of the skies
And on the dark blue serge upon his thighs.

Every time a man the farmer knew
Went by upon the road, the farmer's hound
On the church's wooden porch outside
Would thump his tail and make a pleasant sound,
His tail struck every time that it went round.

The farmer knew how well he knew each friend
Going by, he counted up the score;
If the passer-by were a plain friend,
There would be three thumps, or maybe four,
But if it was a good friend, it was more.

That would be Sam Rogers passing now,
And that would be Dave Merryman, all right,
For the hound-dog's joy flowed down his tail
And made it pound the planks with all its might,
He could not stop it going for delight.

The man in church sat back and glowed all
    through,

He heard the sermon, but it did not hide
The rhythm of the comforting old hymn
Of friendship that was going on outside,
And every inch of him filled out with pride.

ROBERT P. TRISTRAM COFFIN

Old Blue

I had a dog and his name was Blue,
And I betcha five dollars he's a good dog too.
Saying, "Come on, Blue, you good dog, you."

Shouldered my axe and I tooted my horn,
Gonna get me a possum in the new-ground corn.
"Go on, Blue, I'm comin' too."

Chased that possum up a 'simmon tree;
Blue looked at the possum, possum looked at me,
Saying, "Go on, Blue, you can have some too."

Baked that possum good and brown,
Laid them sweet potatoes 'round and 'round,
Saying, "Come on, Blue, you can have some too."

"Blue, what makes your eyes so red?"
"I've run them possums till I'm almost dead."
"Go on, Blue, I'm comin' too."

Old Blue died, and he died so hard
That he dug little holes in my backyard,
Saying, "Go on, Blue, I'm comin' too."

I dug his grave with a silver spade,
And I let him down with a golden chain,
Saying, "Go on, Blue, I'm comin' too."

When I get to Heaven, first thing I'll do,
Grab my horn, and I'll blow for old Blue.
Saying, "Come on, Blue, finally got here too."

AMERICAN FOLK SONG

The Woodman's Dog

Shaggy, and lean, and shrewd, with pointed ears
And tail cropped short, half lurcher and half cur—
His dog attends him. Close behind his heel
Now creeps he slow; and now with many a frisk
Wide-scampering, snatches up the drifted snow
With ivory teeth, or plows it with his snout;
Then shakes his powdered coat and barks for joy.

WILLIAM COWPER

Stop Kicking My Dog Around

Every time I come to town
The boys keep kicking my dog around;
Even if he is a hound
They've got to stop kicking my dog around!

AMERICAN FOLK SONG

THEIR DOGGINESS

"The Power of the Dog"

There is sorrow enough in the natural way
From men and women to fill our day;
And when we are certain of sorrow in store,
Why do we always arrange for more?
Brothers and Sisters, I bid you beware
Of giving your heart to a dog to tear.

Buy a pup and your money will buy
Love unflinching that cannot lie—
Perfect passion and worship fed
By a kick in the ribs or a pat on the head.
Nevertheless it is hardly fair
To risk your heart for a dog to tear.

When the fourteen years which Nature permits
Are closing in asthma, or tumor, or fits,
And the vet's unspoken prescription runs
To lethal chambers or loaded guns,
Then you will find—it's your own affair—
But . . . you've given your heart to a dog to tear.

When the body that lived at your single will,
With its whimper of welcome, is stilled (how
    still!).

When the spirit that answered your every mood
Is gone—wherever it goes—for good,
You will discover how much you care,
And will give your heart to a dog to tear.

We've sorrow enough in the natural way,
When it comes to burying Christian clay.
Our loves are not given, but only lent,
At compound interest of cent per cent.
Though it is not always the case, I believe,
That the longer we've kept 'em, the more do we
    grieve:
For, when debts are payable, right or wrong,
A short-time loan is as bad as a long—
So why in—Heaven (before we are there)
Should we give our hearts to a dog to tear?

RUDYARD KIPLING

Me and Samantha

Samantha the golden retriever
Lies at the edge of the grass,
Prepared for her favorite pastime,
Which is barking at persons who pass.

Her owners insist she's just friendly,
And I guess that I would agree.
But some people don't care for barkers,
And one of those people is me.

Yet when I go out in the morning
And when I come back around dark,
Samantha is lying there waiting
To run up and greet me, and bark.

Samantha, I've been an admirer
Of yours since you were a pup,
But I know I would like you much better,
If you'd be a good girl, and shut up.

PYKE JOHNSON, JR.

Night Song

On moony nights the dogs bark shrill
Down the valley and up the hill.

There's one who is angry to behold
The moon so unafraid and cold,
That makes the earth as bright as day,
But yet unhappy, dead, and grey.

Another in his strawy lair,
Says: "Who's a-howling over there?
By heavens I will stop him soon
From interfering with the moon."

So back he barks, with throat upthrown;
"You leave our moon, our moon alone."
And other distant dogs respond
Beyond the fields, beyond, beyond.

FRANCES CORNFORD

Dog Around the Block

Dog around the block, sniff,
Hydrant sniffing, corner, grating,
Sniffing, always, starting forward,
Backward, dragging, sniffing backward,
Leash at taut, leash at dangle,
Leash in people's feet entangle—
Sniffing dog, apprised of smellings,
Love of life, and fronts of dwellings,
Meeting enemies,
Loving old acquaintance, sniff,
Sniffing hydrant for reminders,

Leg against the wall, raise,
Leaving grating, corner greeting,
Chance for meeting, sniff, meeting,
Meeting, telling, news of smelling,
Nose to tail, tail to nose,
Rigid, careful, pose,
Liking, partly liking, hating,
Then another hydrant, grating,
Leash at taut, leash at dangle,
Tangle, sniff, untangle,
Dog around the block, sniff.

E. B. WHITE

Tom's Little Dog

Tom told his dog called Tim to beg,
And up at once he sat,
His two clear amber eyes fixed fast,
His haunches on his mat.

Tom poised a lump of sugar on
His nose; then, "Trust!" says he;
Stiff as a guardsman sat his Tim;
Never a hair stirred he.

"Paid for!" says Tom; and in a trice
Up jerked that moist black nose;
A snap of teeth, a crunch, a munch,
And down the sugar goes!

WALTER DE LA MARE

Lost Dog

He lifts his hopeful eyes at each new tread,
Dark wells of brown with half his heart in each;
He will not bark, because he is well-bred,
Only one voice can heal the sorry breach.
He scans the faces that he does not know,
One paw uplifted, ear cocked for a sound
Outside his sight. Only he must not go
Away from here; by honor he is bound.
Now he has heard a whistle down the street;
He trembles in a sort of ecstasy,
Dances upon his eager, padding feet,
Straining himself to hear, to feel, to see,
And rushes at a call to meet the one
Who of his tiny universe is sun.

FRANCES RODMAN

Pete at the Seashore

i ran along the yellow sand
and made the sea gulls fly
i chased them down the waters edge
i chased them up the sky

i ran so hard i ran so fast
i left the spray behind
i chased the flying flecks of foam
and i outran the wind

an airplane sailing overhead
climbed when it heard me bark
i yelped and leapt right at the sun
until the sky grew dark

some little children on the beach
threw sticks and ran with me
o master let us go again
and play beside the sea

DON MARQUIS

Contentment

I like the way that the world is made,
   (Tickle me, please, behind the ears)
With part in the sun and part in the shade
   (Tickle me, *please*, behind the ears).
This comfortable spot beneath a tree
Was probably planned for you and me;
Why *do* you suppose God made a flea?
Tickle me more behind the ears.

I hear a cricket or some such bug
   (Tickle me, please, behind the ears)
And there is a hole some creature dug
   (Tickle me, *please*, behind the ears).
I can't quite smell it from where we sit,
But I think a rabbit would hardly fit;
Tomorrow, perhaps, I'll look into it:
   Tickle me more behind the ears.

A troublesome fly is near my nose,
   (Tickle me, please, behind the ears);
He thinks I'll snap at him, I suppose,
   (Tickle me, *please*, behind the ears).
If I lay on my back with my legs in air
Would you scratch my stomach, just here and
     there?
It's a puppy trick and I don't much care,
   But tickle me more behind the ears.

54

Heaven, I guess, is all like this
   (Tickle me, please, behind the ears);
It's my idea of eternal bliss
   (Tickle me, *please*, behind the ears).
With angel cats for a dog to chase,
And a very extensive barking space,
And big bones buried all over the place,—
   And you, to tickle behind my ears.

BURGES JOHNSON

Dog, Midwinter

This dog barking at me now—
do I really bother him
or is he acting out
the old faithful watch-dog routine?

Or (and I hope it's this)
is he so lonely locked up
in the snow-filled yard that the sight
of another living thing stirs him?

For I can truly say
I'm as lonely now

as you, dog, so
speaking for both of us
bark your crazy head off.

RAYMOND SOUSTER

Two Dogs Have I

For years we've had a little dog,
Last year we acquired a big dog;
He wasn't big when we got him,
He was littler than the dog we had.
We thought our little dog would love him,
Would help him to become a trig dog,
But the new little dog got bigger,
And the old little dog got mad.

Now the big dog loves the little dog,
But the little dog hates the big dog,
The little dog is eleven years old,
And the big dog only one;
The little dog calls him *Schweinhund,*
The little dog calls him Pig-dog,
She grumbles broken curses
As she dreams in the August sun.

56

The big dog's teeth are terrible,
But he wouldn't bite the little dog;
The little dog wants to grind his bones,
But the little dog has no teeth;
The big dog is acrobatic,
The little dog is a brittle dog;
She leaps to grip his jugular,
And passes underneath.

The big dog clings to the little dog
Like glue and cement and mortar;
The little dog is his own true love;
But the big dog is to her
Like a scarlet rag to a Longhorn,
Or a suitcase to a porter;
The day he sat on the hornet
I distinctly heard her purr.

Well, how can you blame the little dog
Who was once the household darling?
He romps like a young Adonis,
She droops like an old mustache;
No wonder she steals his corner,
No wonder she comes out snarling,
No wonder she calls him *Cochon*
And even *Espèce de vache*.

Yet once I wanted a sandwich,
Either caviar or cucumber,

When the sun had not yet risen
And the moon had not yet sank;
As I tiptoed through the hallway
The big dog lay in slumber,
And the little dog slept by the big dog,
And her head was on his flank.

OGDEN NASH

Unsatisfied Yearning

Down in the silent hallway
    Scampers the dog about,
And whines, and barks, and scratches,
    In order to get out.

Once in the glittering starlight,
    He straightway doth begin
To set up a doleful howling
    In order to get in!

RICHARD KENDALL MUNKITTRICK

Silly Dog

There she is, out in the rain,
My silly old dog come back again

To whine and whimper and lick my hands,
Telling me that she understands

That it's better to stay where it's warm and dry,
Not to go fighting with a sky

Spilling over with cold and wet.
But I know when it rains again, she'll forget,

And she'll bark and beg to go out again
To try and outsmart the pouring rain.

MYRA COHN LIVINGSTON

Hope

At the foot of the stairs
my black dog sits;
in his body,
out of his wits.

On the other side
of the shut front door

there's a female dog
he's nervous for.

She's the whole size
of his mind—immense.
Hope ruling him
past sense.

WILLIAM DICKEY

A Dog

I am alone.
Someone is raking leaves
outside
and there is one yellow leaf
on the black branch
brushing the window.

Suddenly a wet cold nose
nuzzles
my empty hand.

CHARLOTTE ZOLOTOW

60

The Bath

Hang garlands on the bathroom door;
  Let all the passages be spruce;
For, lo, the victim comes once more,
  And, ah, he struggles like the deuce!

Bring soaps of many scented sorts;
  Let girls in pinafores attend,
With John, their brother, in his shorts,
  To wash their dusky little friend.

Their little friend, the dusky dog,
  Short-legged and very obstinate,
Faced like a much-offended frog,
  And fighting hard against his fate.

Vain are his protests—in he goes.
  His young barbarians crowd around;
They soap his paws, they soap his nose;
  They soap wherever fur is found.

And soon, still laughing, they extract
  His limpness from the darkling tide;
They make the towel's roughness act
  On back and head and dripping side.

They shout and rub and rub and shout—
  He deprecates their odious glee—
Until at last they turn him out,
  A damp, gigantic bumble-bee.

Released, he barks and rolls, and speeds
From lawn to lawn, from path to path,
And in one glorious minute needs
More soapsuds and another bath.

R. C. LEHMANN

DOG TALES

A Village Tale

Why did the woman want to kill one dog?
Perhaps he was too lively, made her nervous,
A vivid terrier, restless, always barking,
And so unlike the gentle German shepherd.
She did not know herself what demon seized her,
How in the livid afternoon she was possessed,
What strength she found to tie a heavy stone
Around his neck and drown him in the horse-
    trough,
Murder her dog. God knows what drove her to it,
What strength she found to dig a shallow grave
And bury him—her own dog!—in the garden.

And all this while the gentle shepherd watched,
Said nothing, anxious nose laid on his paws,
Tail wagging dismal questions, watched her go
Into the livid afternoon outside to tire
The demon in her blood with wine and gossip.
The gate clanged shut, and the good shepherd ran,
Ran like a hunter to the quarry, hackles raised,
Sniffed the loose earth on the haphazard grave,
Pressing his eager nose into the dust,
Sensed tremor there and (frantic now) dug fast,
Dug in, dug in, all shivering and whining,

Unearthed his buried friend, licked the dry nose
Until a saving sneeze raised up the dead.

Well, she had to come back sometime to face
Whatever lay there waiting, worse than horror:
Two wagging tails, four bright eyes shifting—
Moment of truth, and there was no escape.
She could face murder. Could she face redeeming?
Was she relieved? Could she perhaps pretend
It had not really happened after all?
All that the village sees is that the dog
Sits apart now, untouchable and sacred,
Lazarus among dogs, whose loving eyes
Follow her back and forth until she dies.
She gives him tidbits. She can always try
To make them both forget the murderous truth.

But he knows and she knows that they are bound
Together in guilt and mercy, world without end.

MAY SARTON

Dog in the Fountain

Just as the day is about to die
at 8:41 of a dull September morning,
a scrawny, looking-like-nothing dog
appears from nowhere on University Avenue,
runs three or four steps up to the Courthouse foun-
    tain,
jumps another step into the cold seething water,
and plunges, tosses, drinks, gurgles his way across
    it,
then back again to show it's not an accident,
and out with a series of shakes, and me shaking,
    dripping with him,
as the day suddenly changes its mind,
lets itself be born over again.

RAYMOND SOUSTER

Beth-Gêlert

The spearmen heard the bugle sound,
And cheerily smiled the morn;
And many a brach, and many a hound
Obeyed Llewellyn's horn.

And still he blew a louder blast,
And gave a lustier cheer,
"Come, Gêlert, come, wert never last
Llewellyn's horn to hear.

"O where does faithful Gêlert roam
The flower of all his race;
So true, so brave—a lamb at home,
A lion in the chase?"

In sooth, he was a peerless hound,
The gift of royal John;
But now no Gêlert could be found,
And all the chase rode on.

That day Llewellyn little loved
The chase of hart and hare;
And scant and small the booty proved,
For Gêlert was not there.

Unpleased, Llewellyn homeward hied,
When, near the portal seat,
His truant Gêlert he espied
Bounding his lord to greet.

But when he gained the castle-door,
Aghast the chieftain stood;
The hound all o'er was smeared with gore;
His lips, his fangs, ran blood.

Llewellyn gazed with fierce surprise;
Unused such looks to meet,
His favorite checked his joyful guise,
And crouched, and licked his feet.

Onward, in haste, Llewellyn passed,
And on went Gêlert too;
And still, where'er his eyes he cast,
Fresh blood-gouts shocked his view.

O'erturned his infant's bed he found,
With blood-stained covert rent;
And all around the walls and ground
With recent blood besprent.

He called his child—no voice replied—
He searched with terror wild;
Blood, blood he found on every side,
But nowhere found his child.

"Hell-hound! my child's by thee devoured,"
The frantic father cried;
And to the hilt his vengeful sword
He plunged in Gêlert's side.

Aroused by Gêlert's dying yell,
Some slumberer wakened nigh;
What words the parent's joy could tell
To hear his infant's cry!

Concealed beneath a tumbled heap
His hurried search had missed
All glowing from his rosy sleep
The cherub boy he kissed.

Nor scathe had he, nor harm, nor dread,
But, the same couch beneath,
Lay a gaunt wolf, all torn and dead,
Tremendous still in death.

Ah, what was then Llewellyn's pain!
For now the truth was clear;
His gallant hound the wolf had slain.
To save Llewellyn's heir.

WILLIAM ROBERT SPENCER

The Diners in the Kitchen

Our dog Fred
Et the bread.

Our dog Dash
Et the hash.

Our dog Pete
Et the meat.

70

Our dog Davy
Et the gravy.

Our dog Toffy
Et the coffee.

Our dog Jake
Et the cake.

Our dog Trip
Et the dip.

And—the worst,
From the first,—

Our dog Fido
Et the pie-dough.

JAMES WHITCOMB RILEY

The Night Hunt

In the morning, in the dark,
When the stars begin to blunt,
By the wall of Barna Park
Dogs I heard and saw them hunt.

All the parish dogs were there,
All the dogs for miles around,
Teeming up behind a hare,
In the dark, without a sound.

How I heard I scarce can tell—
'Twas a patter in the grass—
And I did not see them well
Come across the dark and pass;
Yet I saw them and I knew
Spearman's dog and Spellman's dog
And, beside my own dog too,
Leamy's from the Island Bog.

In the morning when the sun
Burnished all the green to gorse,
I went out to take a run
Round the bog upon my horse;
And my dog that had been sleeping
In the heat beside the door
Left his yawning and went leaping
On a hundred yards before.

Through the village street we passed—
Not a dog there raised a snout—
Through the street and out at last
On the white bog road and out
Over Barna Park full pace,
Over to the Silver Stream,

Horse and dog in happy race,
Rider between thought and dream.

By the stream at Leamy's house,
Lay a dog—my pace I curbed—
But our coming did not rouse
Him from drowsing undisturbed;
And my dog, as unaware
Of the other, dropped beside
And went running by me there
With my horse's slackened stride.

Yet by something, by a twitch
Of the sleeper's eye, a look
From the runner, something which
Little chords of feeling shook,
I was conscious that a thought
Shuddered through the silent deep
Of a secret—I had caught
Something I had known in sleep.

THOMAS MACDONAGH

from **A Dog in the Quarry**

The day was so bright
    that even birdcages flew open.
The breasts of lawns
    heaved with joy
and the cars on the highway
    sang the great song of asphalt.
At Lobzy a dog fell in the quarry
    and howled.
Mothers pushed their prams out of the park oppo-
    site
because babies cannot sleep
    when a dog howls,
and a fat old pensioner was cursing the Munici-
    pality:
  they let the dog fall in the quarry and then leave
    him there,
and this, if you please, has been going on since
    morning.

Toward evening even the trees
    stopped blossoming
and the water at the bottom of the quarry
    grew green with death.
But still the dog howled.

Then along came some boys
and made a raft out of two logs
and two planks.
And a man left on the bank
a briefcase . . .
he laid aside his briefcase
and sailed with them.

Their way led across a green puddle
to the island where the dog waited.
It was a voyage like
      the discovery of America,
a voyage like
      the quest of Theseus.

The dog fell silent,
      the boys stood like statues
and one of them punted with a stick,
the waves shimmered nervously,
tadpoles swiftly
      flickered out of the wake,
the heavens
      stood still,
and the man stretched out his hand.

It was a hand
      reaching out across the ages,
it was a hand

linking
one world with another,
life with death,
it was a hand
joining everything together,
it caught the dog by the scruff of its neck

and then they sailed back
to the music of
an immense fanfare
of the dog's yapping . . .

MIROSLAV HOLUB

*Translated from the Czechoslovakian
by George Theiner and Ian Milner*

The Dog's Cold Nose

When Noah, perceiving 'twas time to embark,
Persuaded the creatures to enter the Ark,
The dog, with a friendliness truly sublime,
Assisted in herding them. Two at a time
He drove in the elephants, zebras and gnus
Until they were packed like a boxful of screws,
The cat in the cupboard, the mouse on the shelf,
The bug in the crack; then he backed in himself.
But such was the lack of available space
He couldn't tuck all of him into the place;

So after the waters had flooded the plain
And down from the heavens fell blankets of rain
He stood with his muzzle thrust out through the
    door
The whole forty days of that terrible pour!
Because of which drenching, zoologists hold,
The nose of a healthy dog always is cold!

ARTHUR GUITERMAN

Elegy on the Death of a Mad Dog

Good people all, of every sort,
Give ear unto my song;
And if you find it wondrous short,
It cannot hold you long.

In Islington there was a man,
Of whom the world might say,
That still a godly race he ran,
Whene'er he went to pray.

A kind and gentle heart he had,
To comfort friends and foes;
The naked every day he clad,
When he put on his clothes.

And in that town a dog was found,
As many dogs there be,
Both mongrel, puppy, whelp, and hound,
And curs of low degree.

This dog and man at first were friends;
But when a pique began,
The dog, to gain some private ends,
Went mad and bit the man.

Around from all the neighbouring streets
The wondering neighbours ran,
And swore the dog had lost his wits,
To bite so good a man.

The wound it seem'd both sore and sad
To every Christian eye;
And while they swore the dog was mad,
They swore the man would die.

But soon a wonder came to light,
That show's the rogues they lied:
The man recover'd of the bite,
The dog it was that died.

OLIVER GOLDSMITH

Sudden Assertion

I watched the house, and barked agreeably, and
    wagged my tail, and ran to pick up sticks
you threw with such a gesture!
You liked me when I grinned my wide approval,
although there was a red light in my eye
that made you wonder . . . and I slavered so!
Anyway, now you know,
you and the tender lambies,
now you know!

KENNETH LESLIE

The Turkish Trench Dog

Night held me as I scrawled and scrambled near
The Turkish lines. Above, the mocking stars
Silvered the curving parapet, and clear
Cloud-latticed beams o'erflecked the land with
    bars;
I, crouching, lay between
Tense-listening armies, peering through the night,
Twin giants bound by tentacles unseen.
Here in dim-shadowed light
I saw him, as a sudden movement turned
His eyes towards me, glowing eyes that burned
A moment ere his snuffling muzzle found

79

My trail; and then as serpents mesmerize
He chained me with those unrelenting eyes,
That muscle-sliding rhythm, knit and bound
In spare-limbed symmetry, those perfect jaws
And soft-approaching pitter-patter paws.
Nearer and nearer like a wolf he crept—
That moment had my swift revolver leapt—
But terror seized me, terror born of shame,
Brought brooding revelation. For he came
As one who offers comradeship deserved,
An open ally of the human race,
And sniffling at my prostrate form unnerved
He licked my face!

GEOFFREY DEARMER

MUTTS

Mick

Mick my mongrel-O
Lives in a bungalow,
Painted green with a round doorway.
With an eye for cats
And a nose for rats
He lies on his threshold half the day.
He buries his bones
By the rockery stones,
And never, oh never, forgets the place.
Ragged and thin
From his tail to his chin,
He looks at you with a sideways face.
Dusty and brownish,
Wicked and clownish,
He'll win no prize at the County Show.
But throw him a stick,
And up jumps Mick,
And right through the flower-beds see him go!

JAMES REEVES

The Dollar Dog

A dollar dog is all mixed up.
A bit of this, a bit of that.
We got ours when he was a pup
So small he slept in an old hat.
So small we borrowed a doll's beads
To make him his first collar.
Too small to see how many breeds
We got for just one dollar.
But not at all too small to see
He had an appetite.
An appetite? It seems to me
He ate up everything in sight!
The more he ate, the more we saw.
He got to be as big as two.
The more we saw, the more we knew
We had a genuine drooly-jaw,
Mishmash mongrel, all-around,
Flop-eared, bull-faced, bumble-paw,
Stub-tailed, short-haired, Biscuit Hound.

JOHN CIARDI

A Man in Our Village

A man in our village,
a village high in the hills,
often among clouds,
a poor village with little money,
this man had a dog.

She was not a pretty dog.
Her coat was unkempt black and tan
and she was small and thin.
You wouldn't have looked twice at her—
unless you had noticed how closely
she stayed beside the man,
watching his every step, staying
close to his heels, watching him.
It was clear she loved the man.

The dog's eyes were brown
and very, very bright. Her name
was Betsy. Someone told me that.
I never heard anyone call her by name,
nobody patted her or fondled her ears.
Once a child bent down to speak to her
where she sat near the man
as he spoke to a friend in the street.
But she growled quietly, not in anger,
just to say she didn't want to be spoken to.
The man was just a man.

There was a high path over the hills,
a short cut to the next valley.
One day people saw the man and his dog
walk out along the path. It was winter,
the hill pools had been solid ice for a month,
the ground was as hard as a bone.
The man vanished around a bend
and his dog was as frail behind him
as his winter shadow. And soon it grew dark.

Not only evening dark, not only the natural dusk.
Clouds heavy with snow grew bleakly under the
    moon
and in an hour the hills, the village,
the white countryside, all lay under the muffling
snow. All night it fell. Everything
was altered. All paths were hidden under
that fallen sky. We began to worry
about the man and his little dog.

In the morning we set out over the changed hills,
in a long line, calling one to the other,
to keep in touch. Blue shadows filled
the hollows, and we swung our arms in the cold
and we shouted. All morning we searched
but we did not find them, nor any sign of them.

A bitter wind filled our eyes with tears
and we moved slowly, with great weariness,

through the deep snow. We gave up hope.
We stumbled back along the tracks we had made.

But a great shout stopped us. They were found!
We knew they were found by the joy
of the loud call, by the waving of arms
near a crop of rocks. They lay under
what shelter the rocks could have given them
and they were alive. The man could not hear us,
he was insensible with cold. But his little dog
had crept and curled herself over his heart
and kept him warm. She had saved his life.
We brought them down, step by step, through
        snow,
and into a house blazing with comfort.
We praised the little dog, made much of her,
gave her warm milk to drink, for the first time
spoke her name.

When summer came again and the hills
turned kind and pink with heather,
the man sold his dog to a passing visitor.
He sold her, although she had saved his life.
Would you have done that, would you?
I didn't think anyone could have done that.

LESLIE NORRIS

Dogs of Santiago

Do not be a lost dog
in Santiago—
lost dogs in Santiago
trot forever
through the day
and through the night
they trot from shadow into light
and back to shadow
through winter, spring, summer, and fall
looking neither left or right
no longer knowing door from door
insensitive to track or spoor—
never breaking pace

Be a pit bull
pull carts
run a water wheel
join the canine corps
chase the wolf
or the wild boar
herd cattle or guard sheep
accept the kennel and the leash
if you must
work for police
betray partridge and quail

but do not fail
and become a lost dog
trotting through the streets
of Santiago

EUGENE MCCARTHY

The Dog

The dog was there, outside her door,
   She gave it food and drink,
She gave it shelter from the cold:
   It was the night young Molly robbed
An old fool of his gold.

"Molly," I said, "you'll go to hell—"
   And yet I half believed
That ugly, famished, tottering cur
   Would bark outside the gates of Heaven,
To open them for Her!

W. H. DAVIES

THOROUGHBREDS

Whippet

His head is tiny because he has few brains.
Flesh wraps his limbs like paper round a stick.
He is a trembling creature, made of fear,
Forever crawling into cosy places,
Shivering at a puff; a dustbin scavenger,
Vomiting rubbish that he can't resist.
The fool can even fall off beds and sofas.
His chest's so deep he can't get under gates,
So narrow that he can't lie down on it.
Give him a woodland walk, he'll come back
    bloody,
Skin torn by twigs and stalks, like tissue paper.
His ears are limp, his sense of smell is comic.
His favourite feast is rind of cucumber.
He cannot sleep alone, the darkness scares him.

Dead loss? Not worth his licence? Just a nuisance?

Carry him to the common. Set him down.
Shout "Go, boy, go," clap hands, excite the air.
He watches you, shaking, with his whiteless eyes,
Forelegs stretched straight as matchsticks, parallel,
His back legs folded under his bony bottom.
He trembles, shudders, shrinks, lays back his ears,

Swivels his eyeballs, hides his naked tail.
"Run, boy! Shift your arse, boy! Damn you, run!"
And suddenly a hidden spring goes snap
And catapults him into space—he's off!
Now out of pantomime bursts poetry,
Dazzling, enrapturing, a miracle.
Blood rockets through your heart as round he flies.
You marvel, too bewitched to understand
The transformation of this bag of bones.
You spin and stamp and shout, too thrilled to
    wonder
—As he wings past, a foot above the ground—
How such a freak can be so beautiful.

PRUDENCE ANDREW

The Bloodhound

I am the dog world's best detective.
My sleuthing nose is so effective
I sniff the guilty at a distance
And then they lead a doomed existence.
My well-known record for convictions
Has earned me lots of maledictions
From those whose trail of crime I scented

And sent to prison, unlamented.
Folks either must avoid temptation
Or face my nasal accusation.

EDWARD ANTHONY

The Collies

In fiction tales we keep performing
Heroics that are most heart-warming.
We rescue babies left to smother
In burning houses. There's no other
Dog in the world so oft selected
To save the child that's unprotected.
We like that kind of reputation
Because it brings us adoration,
But wish that folks would not forget
We also like the role of pet
And love to stretch out on the floor,
And fall asleep and even snore,
And dream of canine heroes breezy
While we—by collie!—take life easy.

EDWARD ANTHONY

The Dachshund

Because I waddle when I walk,
Should this give rise to silly talk
That I'm ungainly? What's ungainly?
I'm really rather graceful—mainly.
The experts have been known to state
That there's a twinkle in our gait.
One said, "They have a clumsy grace,"
Which after all is no disgrace.

My funny features may abound:
Short legs, long body, low-to-ground,
But I'm about the perfect pal
For man or woman, boy or gal.
I'm gentle, very playful, kind,
I housebreak fast 'cause I'm refined,
I'm smart but never sly or foxy—
No, do not underrate the dachsie!

EDWARD ANTHONY

Best of Show

Wheatfields of chiffon,
Afghans are blown
Into the ring: spunsilk
Waterfall, while

96

Popeyed Chihuahuas
Toothpick about, each
Radar-cocked ear
Plucking news . . . Now

Golden as carp,
Pekinese waddling
On fins of fur,
Whelk tails, swim in;

Next, the Great Danes,
Brindle or pinto,
Sleek as wallpaper,
Enter

Before feathered
English
Setters, time on their
Point to snoot

Most poodles, those
Peacock, tonsured, bright-
Eyed balls of cotton-
Candy; and

Bassetts,
Paws whiter than sneakers,
Map ears their
Epaulettes; or

Weimaraners,
Coats silver
On bacon, yellow
Eyes sly; so different

From Huskies',
Whose Arctic
Look is a squint . . .
These breeds strut till,

Wheezing over its bow-
Legs, a lap
Dog trembles in:
Best of show!

BARBARA HOWES

Fashions in Dogs

An Airedale, erect beside the chauffeur of a Rolls-
 Royce,
Often gives you the impression he's there from
 choice.

In town, the Great Dane
Is kept by the insane.

Today the boxer
Is fashionable and snappy;
But I never saw a boxer
Who looked thoroughly happy.

The Scotty's a stoic,
He's gay and he's mad;
His pace is a snail trot,
His harness is plaid.
I once had a bitch,
Semi-invalid, crazy:
There ne'er was a Scotch girl
Quite like Daisy.

Pekes
Are biological freaks.
They have no snout
And their eyes come out.
Ladies choose'm
To clutch to their bosom.
A Pekinese would gladly fight a wolf or a cougar
But is usually owned by a Mrs. Applegate Krueger.

Cockers are perfect for Elizabeth Barrett Browning,
Or to carry home a package from the A. & P. with-
out clowning.

The wire-haired fox
Is hard on socks
With or without clocks.

The smooth-haired variety
Has practically vanished from nice society,
And it certainly does irk us
That you never see one except when you go to the
        circus.

The dachshund's affectionate,
He wants to wed with you:
Lie down to sleep,
And he's in bed with you.
Sit in a chair,
He's there.
Depart,
You break his heart.

My Christmas will be a whole lot wetter and mer-
        rier
If somebody sends me a six-weeks-old Boston ter-
        rier.

Sealyhams have square sterns and cute faces
Like toy dogs you see at Macy's.
But the Sealyham, while droll in appearance,
Has no clearance.

Chows come in black, and chows come in red;
They could come in bright green, I wouldn't turn
        my head.
The roof of their mouth is supposed to be blue,
Which is one of those things that might easily be
        true.

To us it has never seemed exactly pleasant
To see a beautiful setter on East Fifty-seventh
    Street looking for a woodcock or a pheasant.

German shepherds are useful for leading the blind,
And for biting burglars and Consolidated Edison
    men in the behind.

Lots of people have a rug.
Very few have a pug.

E. B. WHITE

Beagles

Over rock and wrinkled ground
Ran the lingering nose of hound,
The little and elastic hare
Stretched herself nor stayed to stare.

Stretched herself, and far away
Darted through the chinks of day,
Behind her, shouting out her name,
The whole blind world galloping came.

Over hills a running line
Curled like a whip-lash, fast and fine,

Past me sailed the sudden pack
Along the taut and tingling track.

From the far flat scene each shout
Like jig-saw piece came tumbling out,
I took and put them all together,
And then they turned into a tether.

A tether that held me to the hare
Here, there, and everywhere.

W. R. RODGERS

Of an Ancient Spaniel in Her Fifteenth Year

She was never a dog that had much sense,
Too excitable, too intense,
. But she had the cocker's gift of charm.
She never knew what to do with a bone,
But shielded all her life from harm
She cost me several years of my own.

Sweet old pooch! These final years
She rubs white chaps and floating ears

In summersweet suburban loam;
Digs, she thinks, a final home:
Scoops every day fresh graves to lie,
Humble and contented, knowing
Where, any day now, she'll be going—
And so do I.

I said, buying with Christmas care,
Her collar and tag for '49:
This is the last she'll ever wear
(And the same is true of mine).
Equal mercy, and equal dark
Await us both, eternally,
But I was always ready to bark—
And so was she.

CHRISTOPHER MORLEY

The Irish Wolf-Hound

As fly the shadows o'er the grass
   He flies with step as light and sure,
He hunts the wolf through Tostan pass
   And starts the deer by Lisanoure.
The music of the Sabbath bells,

O Con! has not a sweeter sound
Than when along the valley swells
   The cry of John MacDonnell's hound.

His stature tall, his body long,
   His back like night, his breast like snow,
His foreleg pillar-like and strong,
   His hind leg like a bended bow,
Rough curling hair, head long and thin,
   His ear a leaf so small and round,—
Not Bran, the favorite dog of Fin,
   Could rival John MacDonnell's hound.

DENIS FLORENCE MCCARTHY

The Dog Parade

In times of calm or hurricane, in days of sun or
      shower,
The dog-paraders, each and all, observe the canine
      hour,

And, some with pups in single leash, and some
      with tugging pairs,
Take out their poodles, pointers, Poms and frisky
      wirehairs.

The Scotties patter doggedly, sedate and wistful-
   eyed,
The setters leap, the spaniels romp, the Great
   Danes walk in pride.

And here are shaggy shepherd dogs, those heroes
   of the farm,
And there a Russian wolfhound comes with
   quaint, Slavonic charm.

Or one may note a brindled bull, less frivolous
   than most,
Who, like a faithful sentinel, is ever at his post.

But still the dog-paraders march, exchanging
   friendly bows,
Escorting dachshunds, Dobermans, Dalmatians,
   Pekes and chows.

And still in placid dignity that nothing can dis-
   turb,
They lead their charges down the street, and some-
   times to the curb.

                                        ARTHUR GUITERMAN

TRIBUTES

Denise

Come here, Denise!
Come let us find a little patch of sun
And meditate a measurement of time.

I have outlived five dogs:
Hector and Hercules,
Genghis the golden,
The fashionable Pamplemousse,
And, lately, Hans of Weimar,
Hans of the amber eyes.

You are my last, Denise;
Life is but one dog more,
Denise, my raisin-bread Dalmatian,
Denise of the delicate crossed paws.

ROBERT BEVERLY HALE

Epitaph to a Dog

(On a monument in the garden of Newstead Abbey)

NEAR THIS SPOT
ARE DEPOSITED THE REMAINS
OF ONE
WHO POSSESSED BEAUTY
WITHOUT VANITY,
STRENGTH WITHOUT INSOLENCE,
COURAGE WITHOUT FEROCITY,
AND ALL THE VIRTUES OF MAN
WITHOUT HIS VICES.

THIS PRAISE, WHICH WOULD BE UNMEANING
FLATTERY
IF INSCRIBED OVER HUMAN ASHES,
IS BUT A JUST TRIBUTE TO THE MEMORY OF
"BOATSWAIN," A DOG
WHO WAS BORN AT NEWFOUNDLAND,
MAY, 1803,
AND DIED AT NEWSTEAD ABBEY
NOV. 18, 1808

When some proud son of man returns to earth,
Unknown to glory, but upheld by birth,
The sculptor's art exhausts the pomp of woe,
And storied urns record who rests below;

When all is done, upon the tomb is seen,
Not what he was, but what he should have been.
But the poor dog, in life the firmest friend,
The first to welcome, foremost to defend,
Whose honest heart is still his master's own,
Who labors, fights, lives, breathes for him alone,
Unhonored falls, unnoticed all his worth,
Denied in heaven the soul he held on earth—
While man, vain insect! hopes to be forgiven,
And claims himself a sole exclusive heaven.
Oh man! thou feeble tenant of an hour,
Debased by slavery, or corrupt by power—
Who knows thee well must quit thee with disgust,
Degraded mass of animated dust!
Thy love is lust, thy friendship all a cheat,
Thy smiles hypocrisy, thy words deceit!
By nature vile, ennobled but by name,
Each kindred brute might bid thee blush for
     shame.
Ye, who perchance behold this simple urn,
Pass on—it honors none you wish to mourn.
To mark a friend's remains these stones arise;
I never knew but one—and there he lies.

LORD BYRON

For a Good Dog

Some dogs are brats,
Aristocrats,
   Or peevish, pampered minions;
But you're the pup
Who wins the cup,
   Deserving heavenly pinions.

And dogs enough
Are timid, gruff,
   Abased or detrimental;
But you're the tike
Whom all men like,
   Courageous, frank and gentle.

And dogs there be
Too wild and free
   For tactful circumspection;
But you are one
Of sense and fun
   With deep and true affection.

Till rabbits bite,
Till cats at night
   No longer hold their pow-wow,
Through good and ill
We'll cherish still
   Our own beloved bow-wow.

ARTHUR GUITERMAN

Our Lucy (1956–1960)

1

Small as a fox and like
a little fox but black,
   our Lucy's white teeth grin
   among the rushes green.

The feathers of her plume
flutter in the warm
   winds that fitfully blow
   from the Gulf of Mexico,

and like a machine-gun
her barking through the pine
   echoes where people have
   set foot on our grove:

"Quiet, Lucy. They
may bring us news today,
   or if thieves they may
   drop something on their way."

2

She was a happy little dog
because she loved three things only,
us and food and to go barking

forth in the world, feathers high:
of these she had a plenty till
the car hit her at Eagle's Bridge;
died without pain in Sally's arms
blood slowly dripping from her jaws,
we buried her with a borrowed shovel
a cairn of stones on the river bank
—she who leaped with joy to greet us
and enlivened us with her lovely spirit,
how suddenly! there she was
and now is not in our empty house.

PAUL GOODMAN

On the Death of Echo
A Favorite Beagle

Silent at last, beneath the silent ground,
Here Echo lives, no unsubstantial sound
Nor babbling mimic—but a Beagle fleet
With drooping ears, keen nose, and nimble feet.
In the glad Chase she raised her merry voice,
And made her namesake of the woods rejoice,
But now dumb Death has chok'd poor Echo's cry
And to no call can Echo more reply—

HARTLEY COLERIDGE

Hector the Dog

Shake hands with Hector the dog, for Hector is
Not as he appears to be. He gives
A false impression by his yellow glare;
His glare is the glare of love, by love he lives.

Hector's well-bred eye is glassy with love;
He sees our presence and sees nothing more.
If locked behind, he will go loudly mad,
Crash through a window or break down the door.

And this has left him as scarred as some old
    courtier
Who carries the seals of devotion on body and
    head.
He is always there. The king complains about it.
But he'll miss him once the old dog's dead.

KATE BARNES

The Dog from Malta

He came from Malta; and Eumêlus says
He had no better dog in all his days.
We called him Bull; he went into the dark.
Along those roads we cannot hear him bark.

TYMNÈS

(Translated from the Greek by Edmund Blunden)

Luath

He was a gash an' faithful tyke
As ever lap a sheugh or dyke.
His honest, sonsie, baws'nt face
Ay gat him friends in ilka place;
His breast was white, his tousie back
Weel clad wi' coat o' glossy black;
His gawsie tail, wi' upward curl,
Hung owre his hurdies wi' a swirl.

ROBERT BURNS

gash: wise
lap a sheugh: leap a ditch
sonsie, baws'nt: sweet face with a white stripe
tousie: rumpled
gawsie: handsome
hurdies: hips

OLD DOGS

Old Dog Tray

The morn of life is past,
And ev'ning comes at last;
  It brings me a dream of a once happy day,
Of merry forms I've seen
Upon the village green,
  Sporting with my old dog Tray.
    Old dog Tray's ever faithful;
      Grief cannot drive him away;
    He's gentle, he is kind,
    I'll never, never find
      A better friend than old dog Tray.

The forms I called my own
Have vanish'd one by one,
  The lov'd ones, the dear ones have all
      pass'd away;
Their happy smiles have flown,
Their gentle voices gone,
  I've nothing left but old dog Tray.
    Old dog Tray's ever faithful;
      Grief cannot drive him away;
    He's gentle, he is kind,
    I'll never, never find
      A better friend than old dog Tray.

When thoughts recall the past,
His eyes are on me cast,
　　I know that he feels what my breaking
　　　　heart would say;
Although he cannot speak,
I'll vainly, vainly seek
　　A better friend than old dog Tray.
　　　　Old dog Tray's ever faithful;
　　　　　　Grief cannot drive him away;
　　　　He's gentle, he is kind,
　　　　I'll never, never find
　　　　　　A better friend than old dog Tray.

STEPHEN FOSTER

The House Dog's Grave
(HAIG, AN ENGLISH BULLDOG)

I've changed my ways a little; I cannot now
Run with you in the evenings along the shore,
Except in a kind of dream; and you, if you dream a
　　moment,
You see me there.

So leave awhile the paw-marks on the front door
Where I used to scratch to go out or in,

120

And you'd soon open; leave on the kitchen floor
The marks of my drinking-pan.

I cannot lie by your fire as I used to do
On the warm stone,
Nor at the foot of your bed; no, all the nights
    through
I lie alone.

But your kind thought has laid me less than six
    feet
Outside your window where firelight so often
    plays,
And where you sit to read—and I fear often griev-
    ing for me—
Every night your lamplight lies on my place.

You, man and woman, live so long, it is hard
To think of you ever dying.
A little dog would get tired, living so long.
I hope that when you are lying

Under the ground like me your lives will appear
As good and joyful as mine.
No, dears, that's too much hope: you are not so
    well cared for
As I have been.

And never have known the passionate undivided
Fidelities that I knew.
Your minds are perhaps too active, too many-
    sided . . .
But to me you were true.

You were never masters, but friends. I was your
    friend.
I loved you well, and was loved. Deep love en-
    dures
To the end and far past the end. If this is my end,
I am not lonely. I am not afraid. I am still yours.

ROBINSON JEFFERS

The Span of Life

The old dog barks backward without getting up.
I can remember when he was a pup.

ROBERT FROST

Old Dog

Waddles after
her mistress
also very old

can't somehow make
those shaky muscles move
any more

but day after day
still raises that sagging belly
on the bandy legs

still performs for one block and back
that agony of movement
the torture of each step

the panting tongue
watery eyes
still at odds with death

defying him
through this poem of pain.

RAYMOND SOUSTER

Sunning

Old Dog lay in the summer sun
Much too lazy to rise and run.
He flapped an ear
At a buzzing fly.
He winked a half open
Sleepy eye,
He scratched himself
On an itching spot,
As he dozed on the porch
Where the sun was hot.
He whimpered a bit
From force of habit
While he lazily dreamed
Of chasing a rabbit.
But Old Dog happily lay in the sun
Much too lazy to rise and run.

JAMES S. TIPPETT

Old Dog

Toward the last in the morning she could not
get up, even when I rattled her pan.
I helped her into the yard, but she stumbled
and fell. I knew it was time.

124

The last night a mist drifted over the fields;
in the morning she would not raise her head—
the far, clear mountains we had walked
surged back to mind.

We looked a slow bargain: our days together
were the ones we already had.
I gave her something the vet had given,
and patted her still, a good last friend.

WILLIAM STAFFORD

HAVE I GOT DOGS!

Have I Got Dogs!

Have I got dogs—pedigreeds and mutts—
So darn many people think I'm nuts!

Look at my silken-haired, spunky Spaniel;
He'd fight a lion—I named him Daniel.

There's my curly-tailed, flat-faced Pug—
He's funny-looking, so I named him Mug.

Then there's my Spitz, with her yappy bark—
She loves to swim, so I named her Mark.

My Boxer's the strongest of all my flock—
He's very tough, so I named him Jock.

That English Bulldog is also tough—
So short-tempered I called him Gruff.

There's nervous Jack, my English Setter,
Who never sets—he's a real go-getter!

My Irish Wolfhound's tall as a pony—
He's so skinny that I named him Bony.

See my Dalmation, her name is Dot—
She's quite an easy dog to spot.

Did you ever see such a handsome Poodle?
She's kind of silly, so I call her Noodle.

Pete is a pink-eyed Pit Bull Terrier,
Who looks quite scarey but couldn't be merrier.

My Peke's the tiniest of all my gang—
I was being funny when I named him Fang.

Take Needle-Nose, my speedy Whippet—
You want to race her? Uh uh—skip it!

There's the Schnauzer—I call her Snappy—
She doesn't make the postman happy!

I think the prettiest dog, by golly,
Is lovely Lassie—of *course* she's a Collie!

That Mongrel's the dumbest of all my mutts—
He's so darned stupid I call him Klutz.

Look at my red-haired Irish Setter—
He's named Rusty, but I could do better.

130

My old Dachshund's an awful crank;
He looks like a hot dog—I call him Frank.

When mealtime comes, it's kind of fun—
I holler "CHOW!" and then I RUN!

WILLIAM COLE

Title Index

Author Index

First Line Index